Claire

Claire

Poems

MARLY YOUMANS

LOUISIANA STATE UNIVERSITY PRESS

Baton Rouge

2004

Cloth
13 12 11 10 09 08 07 06 05 04
5 4 3 2 1
Paper
13 12 11 10 09 08 07 06 05 04
5 4 3 2 1

Designer: Melanie O'Quinn Samaha
Typeface: Bembo
Printer and binder: Thomson Shore, Inc.

Library of Congress Cataloging-in-Publication Data:

Youmans, Marly.
   Claire   :   poems / Marly Youmans.
        p.   cm.
   ISBN 0-8071-2901-1 (cloth : alk. paper) — ISBN 0-8071-2902-X (pbk. :
alk. paper)
   I. Title.
   PS3575.O68C57   2004
   811'.54—dc21

                                                    2003011834

NATIONAL
ENDOWMENT
FOR THE ARTS

This publication is supported in part by a grant from the
National Endowment for the Arts.

for Louis D. Rubin, Jr.

CONTENTS

ACKNOWLEDGMENTS

Grateful thanks is due the editors who accepted or requested these or earlier versions of the following poems for first publication: *Apocalypse:* "Asked of a Sibyl," "Barbarians Among Us"; *Artemis:* "Living in a Dead Friend's House"; *Black Warrior Review:* "Claire Thinks of Edvard's Dreams: 2. Self-portrait at 2:00 A.M.," "Presage"; *Blueline:* "Children of Summer," "Inside the Village Limits," "Lawn Colonized by Orb Spiders," "Rite: Six for the Fears"; *Canto:* "Fort Hays, Kansas," "Upon the First Bathtub in Collins, Georgia"; *Carolina Quarterly:* "The Arabic Lesson," "Claire," "Kateri Tekakwitha," "Lady in a Tower, 1870," "Snow House Stories"; *Cold Mountain Review:* "Adirondack Camp"; *Crescent Review:* "At the Glass Doors"; *Davidson Miscellany:* "Sea Change"; *Green Mountains Review:* "Narrative of a Buried Life"; *Hanging Loose:* "In April," "Letter"; *Intro 8:* "Childbed," ed. George Garrett (Garden City, N.Y.: Anchor Press/Doubleday, 1977); *Laurel Review:* "Ellen Cameron White," "The Locomotive Song," "Missouri Stokes"; *Little Magazine:* "Lethargy at Otter Lake," "Letters from Elsewhere"; *Pembroke Magazine:* "About the Turn of the Leaf," "A Winter's Tale"; *Ploughshares:* "The Cherry Trees"; *Rhino:* "Abandon"; *South Carolina Review:* "Becoming Landscape," "Croft with Cows," "Enchanted Story," "History Report," "Piano Rag," "A Retreat," "Testament of the Paisley Loom-Workers," "Windowmaker"; *Southern Poetry Review:* "Claire Thinks of Edvard's Dreams: 1. The Lonely Ones"; *A Terse Set:* "After Rain"; *Wordsmith:* "Arrowhead."

Second publication and other acknowledgments follow: *Nothing Rich, But Some Things Rare: Poetry in the South in The Black Warrior Review, 1974–1984* (reprint; The Gorgas Oak Press of the University of Alabama, 1984): "Each Time"; *River of Dreams: American Poems from the St. Lawrence Valley* (reprint; Canton, N.Y.: Glover, 1990): "Rite: Six for the Fears"; *A Terse Set* (anthology; Providence: Windfall Press): "Fort Hays,

Kansas," "History Report," "In April," "The Lonely Ones." "The Lonely Ones" and "Self-portrait at 2:00 A.M." were part of a group of poems that won the Gertrude Claytor Prize of the Academy of American Poets, Hollins College. Thanks are due the Virginia Center for the Creative Arts for a fellowship, during which some of these poems were written.

Claire

SNOW HOUSE STORIES

To Michael

Our district's bedtime tales of snow are cruel.
The steps of toddlers, moving back and forth
Between two doors, the sled runs to a pond.

At Mirror Lake a woman slipped through ice
And drank the cold. In blue twilight she saw
Lucent souls of lost unlucky children

Suspended in the ice, or floating past
In sodden hoods and gowns, unharmed by smiles
Of pike. Claire spoke; then she forgot all words.

The man detected nothing. Logged, his sleeve
Now strained in silence that the blackbirds fled.
He felt the world attending as he fished.

Next he could feel the stars kneel at his back.
And he could feel the planets stare to think.
Then particles were getting in his eyes.

And afterward he proved the orphic voice
To be a kind of choking, stop and start.
The leastmost tendril crept across his wrist.

She didn't want to come. She didn't want
That birth. Claire wanted nothing. Still, she was
Upraised by hair from water's placid womb.

It seemed there was no link with nature's dark.
And after all, she lived. The neighbors sprang
From shining homes to help him lift her forth.

The snow kept on, tireless, wide spaced as stars.

Claire

Lepidopteran

Like shards of moon that jag and flash from grass,
Glowing cloudywing and cloudless sulphur
Float on air. Her summer lawns see flight's pure
Syllables: *atala, thula, anise.*

Now lyrical uprisings create moon,
And now a tor of darkness mounts the fir,
While on light hearts begin to stamp and burn
The dervishes of night, death's head, luna.

But songs that flutter wings in her and rise
Anew to breath of world's frail spiracles
Are not so white and cool as butterflies
That gather in their lunar miracles,

Nor are so strange with passion as to batter
And singe against a filament of flame,
But now are tipped with fiery flakes that scatter,
And now are warm and fair and without blame.

THE ARABIC LESSON

For Leila Amal

Clear green flies mating in the bamboo leaves,
Everything as in a Japanese
Poem, the lees
In a glass, curtain trailing
Its far perfume . . .
The children from next door
Were leaning in the leafiest places,
Straight bodies growing curved—their longings streamed
Past sliding doors.
The children taught:

Say *riha,* say *amar, hilal,* the words
As useless as the spinning sands, but Claire
Said them to hold
The feckless flies that bred
In air, *d'ow*
That languished on the leaves,
The great, greeny dustjacket of a world
Where somewhere rockets pistoled and ash clouds
Filtered up.
Staring at sift

Of light on leaf, Claire thought of turning thirty
—An end!—some promises in writing made
By a fortune
Cookie, grief of being
No more, no
Better than she should be.
And dreamed a tale of ancient single self,
Toy queen of glass who broke to babel all
These casts of mind,
This sex, this race.

And then Claire looked—the children were leaning,
Who owned more names than she did for the world,
Who taught her *love*
And *really going crazy*

On the same day—
And saw that they would know
No better how to grow than she, who knew
Not the pure, incantatory names
Of *light* and *leaf*
So many ways.

RITE: SIX FOR THE FEARS

That quaking sulphurs and enameled brass
Of dragonflies will fly, that goldenrod,
Its staves now shocked for gathering, will pass,

That Claire will find (beneath a shelf of sod
Alit in fireweed) nests of skulls and snakes,
But furred and tannic—gifts to a bog god,

And that a stream will lap at ferny brakes
With stones and shallows laved by soaking hair
Of girls, its music lost, that creeks and lakes

Go black, that sounds remaining to the air
Will be defiling rasps of insect song
Without a noise of children anywhere,

That he who left her for an hour is gone
For good, and Claire will never have the things
She dreamed of by Grasse River save the one—

And last, when she has nothing else, she'll fling
Herself on wave-worn shillets, dumb to tell
Of all that has been lost and mute to sing.

ARROWHEAD

Claire, her song, no. 1

His sea was ridge and northern meadowland.
Too plumb-stone deep for children—billow, strand,

And foam too wild. By chimneynook it thrummed,
Was tidal where his black-gowned women strummed

The nerves and swam with word-murderous eye.
His sea spat arrowheads from furrowed rye

And millet, harvest points of dead-drab stone,
One of unmoving cloud. His sea, by bone

Inhabited—the spars of swallowed men.
And with no instrument could he begin

To compass its severe and high romance
Or radiant abyss, a gulf of chance

And risk. Yet all the sea was just a fleck
In the eye of God! Above his hopes, a wreck

Of rich cargo, on decks at Arrowhead
This Melville walked the plank. The barrow dead

Don't go so winding-deep in dark as he
Who crafted nets of words, a fate to flee

Or find—this lone Jonah, terribly free
To snatch at God, mankind, the plunging sea.

INSIDE THE VILLAGE LIMITS

Each twilight of our recent moon-drenched nights,
Claire watched the people coming home from work,
Stopping on lawns, on verge of walks to stare
At strangely brief, far northern grass, gone stiff
And spiked with cold, with beads not ice but near.

Below intent wrought radiance of moon,
She saw dew transferred whole to anklebone
And to the gleam of serviceable shoes.
She saw a shoulder slumped as if toward sleep,
A leach of strength, a winter-whispering fear.

As if each one alone had seen the signs.
The dry and weathered shanks of trees were sparked
With crystal, last monarchs bewildered heads
Of autumn blooms, and the gingko let go
Its windless fans all one long yellow day.

Granular snow with numb bacteria
Brooded behind the door. Our sages said,
"It's soon," and cited lunar women snared
Between their youth and age, who wasted hours
In packing and unpacking waning stores.

LAWN COLONIZED BY ORB SPIDERS

Then orb by orb, the netting bounced
In strong mistrals of fall. A catch
Of snared nasturtium blossoms flounced,

And daring Leaf, an acrobat,
Was twiddling by his stem—at dawn
He fell to grief on *Welcome*'s mat.

By noon Claire swept from step to door
The circus leftovers of night,
The flown trapeze and big-top floor.

A Widow lady-of-the-house,
Accustomed to leaf-twitterings,
She yawned, put fires to bed and doused

The lamp, closed shutters on a bower
Of homespun—Spider's tatty lace,
Blot-ballasted like Queen's Anne's flower.

Her castle dozed, exhaling pale
Cloudage, cocooning fit for stars.
She shut *The Book of Fairy Tale*.

A shining thread of astral milk
Befell and gyred around her sleep.
The Widow battened in its silk

And, dimpled, dreamed a Glowworm King
Who filled autumnal she with light
And promised children fair as spring.

CHILDREN OF SUMMER

The flywheels clicked in dandelion and chicory,
Beneath the wound-up stalks that trembled, rocked, and stalled
On cunning springs. The clouds were sliding gossamer
Of seed elf-shot from ghostly silver-tasseled troops.
A blunt bull-headed beetle clambered, trailed his wings,
A fussy fellow, spattering his flecks of noise—
He saved for comedy a few more afternoons
Of sputtering retort and pinwheel flight through bees.
A coming scythe of cold began to cull Claire's lot:
The matted dreadlock tops of clover hung on stems,
And thistles, plush-and-pineapple, grew old and dreamed
A dome of stars. Not many lacy bloomers changed
Their green and crumpled threads into Queen Anne's crochet.
A galaxy of globes, the star-crammed cradle-pods,
And comet tufts of dying August glowed in rooms.
Claire rummaged up a key and cranked a clockwork finch,
Made rabbits drub a drum as cockroach couples danced,
A winter off from sap and song—returning birds
That twist their notes above a tin diddle of bugs.
First snowflakes latched onto the frosted spear and blade,
And on the autumn's rutted passages to fields.
The doors banged shut on summer. Still, the hall of night
Held living gestures, arc of lamplight, curve of arms,
Known voices calling. Claire gave ground. She damned spring joys
To dwindle in a stark toy-box of ice
But let the starlight branches torn with haste from fall
Release their shining seed against all winterkill
And set a hurricane of stars upon the dark.

ADIRONDACK CAMP

Nostalgist Claire crept through the rotten screens
And clambered over gaps to look at scenes

Of dust—the hearths where mammoths could take shelter,
The thrones of forest barons joined from skelter

Of beautifully mangled cedar, stairs
Collapsed against a bole, unlucky bears

On taxidermy mounts. With fingertips
She grazed a wall adorned with birchbark strips—

Scored by names, a careless hoard of tourists.
Nothing left unharmed or saved for purists

Except the sole unspoiled: a drooping room
Of shelves. The bracket fungi climbed its gloom

And disappeared into a ceiling's dark,
Each rung pricked out with rural scapes—an Ark

Becalmed on Azure Mountain, tamaracks
And hunters, loopy loons, stags crowned with racks

Of monstrous form—some scratched with dates years gone,
One light and dry, a month back newly drawn.

But nowhere could Claire find a single trace
Of parcel-laden ladies in that place,

Nor gentlemen with beadwork bags and gun,
Their Mohawk guide and jacklights meant to stun

Unruly deer. She witnessed how the seeps
Had broached a roof and by the means of creeps

And shifts of indirection overthrown
The northern face of local cobblestone.

Yet a guideboat with its layered blisters
—White and blue, a splotch of green—in asters

Maintained its moorings, and the mirrored pines
Continued shimmying their squiggled lines

Of paint. Decay still ruled the woodland floor.
A web was quilled with needles, as before.

But kneeling down beside the brook, Claire guessed,
"If anywhere, then here," and glimpsed unrest

Of rippled strands escaping woven braids,
The flow of life from Adirondack maids

Still snared and murmuring in roil of stream.
This only: she with need to find, found dream.

> *Unraveling, unraveling the hair*
> *Once plaited with a mother's hope and care.*

At the Glass Doors

A girl once flew
Along be-cypressed god-
Forsaken southern roads,
And there in trees, she saw
A golden hearth that flushed
And sleeved the trees in gilt.
A blazing barrow, fit
To praise a queen, the fall
Upraked to high leafcoal—
Alone, no thrall of fire
To shoulder tines and go
Gold-backed into the dark.

As if the black
Might hold a burning core.
Once loving hands set crowns
Of bine and stars on her:
Claire Ann the child. Now look
At thirty years, at ghost-
Shadows that sigh and gasp
Against the sliding doors,
At waterdrops on glass:
These tears that shine like pearls
Go dim, with just a moon
Of milkglass in the trees.

She would not pass
From doors and wander through
The trees, or sink herself
In leaves, for she now knows
Nothing ever happens
Except the wind and creak
Of pines on mooring roots.
She is no queen. In dark
Of ruins chinked with scrub,
Needle is king. Live oak
(Like glass, leafcool) takes veil
To grieve in Spanish shawls.

LETHARGY AT OTTER LAKE

The Hour

Collecting shreds of golden haze,
Bouquets from tulip trees, ghost-blooms
That past a winter bowed by sleet
Now sprang to shavings in her hands,
Claire stooped to pick up sheaths of bark
And husks, branches drained by lichen
And reindeer moss. And saw one deer.

The Glass of Hours

Cold Otter Lake was slow as jade
Till flung in silks over the dam.
And Otter Creek was iced with skin
Of cellophane, pulled taut and tacked.
A salamander drew Claire's glance—
He wriggled on a stone, then drowsed,
And firelet flame grew straight and still.

The Falling Sands

The boughs and sky were steeped in mist
As Claire shook ashes from an urn:
The bone seemed sand, the flakes seemed wings.
The mourners, flocked and golden bars
Of fish, rose to the roof of air,
And mouths received the guest. Host-white,
The morning sun transformed to moon.

MISSOURI STOKES

Claire, her song, no. 2

In May of '63 the Yankees packed
Exchange men home on smallpox boats,
And a boy died with his head in Thomie's lap.
Grey had invaded my Thomie's hair.
It hurt to see him
Grow strong and limber, leave time
Slipping off as I sewed
Band and buttonhole, eased
The round of shoulder,
Clothes to follow rags
Rotten with camp and march.

He was chilled,
Always. I hated
Leaving him for school, desks emptied
Of flourishing country boys
A teacher at seventeen finds
Hard to tame.

The children lifted narrow faces
As I transgressed, set
Childhood on edge
With something bitter. *It is
Whiteness that Yankees love,*
I said, *our pure Decatur cotton,*
And in nightmares they heard
The threshing noise
Of a thousand bobbins, a thousand
Grinding Yankee factories.
The sin: I was witch,
Pinched hearts to grey.

One month had sped
When I clasped my Thomie's hand
So far as the burned mill.
Then I hated
No man or woman

But wished to hurry on
Forever into another country,
A much farther South.

I parted from him under live oaks,
And he trudged on, did not
Look back, and
Then a wall—then
A hundred walls, blue-black,
Rose up between and held dominion.
My face was wet
As I walked slowly to the school,
The very last time
I saw my brother Thomie.

LADY IN A TOWER, 1870

Claire, her song, no. 3

I lean lone from a tower close
To watch the trees go dark as thought
As western wind upwhirls the snow—

Snow-devils melt in ebb and flow
Of tidal silver, river-wrought.
I lean beyond a tower, close

To burdened cloud and winter glow,
A crust of house where soldiers fought
As mad as wind that whirls. The snow

Obscures the tumbled stone below
The walls. In dreams of *was* and *ought*
I lean. And from a tower close

This seems the way all passed: the woe
Of war, of scorching land, harsh-taught.
As western winds upwhirl the snow,

So dreams hurl me in nightmares now
And always. Such a grief we bought!
Lone-leaning from a tower close,

I count the widowed states, the blows
To pride—reproof that came unsought
As western wind. Up whirls the snow,

The tossing spirit. Men bed low
As plotted earth. Our men forgot
My leaning. From a tower close

Dream-shapes disperse, adrift from foe
And love. They gyre in what is not,
As western wind upwhirls the snow.

ELLEN CAMERON WHITE

Claire, her song, no. 4

1. A Neighbor: Children Sang

Morning, and children
Chanted in the broken plum:
Matt White is dead, they sang,
But I, I didn't believe,
Not with Ellen
Wandering the garden,
Not with old Mrs. White
Serving breakfast to high officers
On the sun porch. *No,*
They told her, *detained, free soon.*

Morning, casually
Rising with tight belly from breakfast,
A captain fired a cradle, the baby
Salvaged like a silver spoon
From burning tissue, her mother
A calm eye
Amid weeping.

Afternoon,
They burned Williamson's
Down to the slip
Of his wife's hair in paper
And letters trussed with ribbon.
In the shattered tree, glee-stung children sang:
Matt White is dead.

Firing,
Fierce popping
And cloud over Ash Grove,
The Cameron girls' dark
Watch, barring wild
Dogs from his face,
A moon very bright that evening.
How white their dresses

And one mute face:
Morning, Matt White, the moon
Still white in the sky,
Matt White stiff in his sheet.

2. Ellen Cameron: My Name

Come morning I was sick,
And sister bent to drape
A damp, sweet towel.
The clink of glass: waves,
Rose and ammonia,
Lapped our faces.

Afternoon I was up and an ache
Fissured my head
As I paced our garden, debris
Of sticks, rubble.
I picked persistent
Thyme and sage, nothing
Else, only herbs
Survive the ruined garden.

A young man, buttons
Neat and tight, bone stitched to stay
With thread the shade of *enemy,*
A face handsome,
Peaceable as a faraway time, idle as Sunday
Afternoons in an orchard,
As sisters who wander in long grass,
Waiting for their sweethearts to climb a slope,
The Indian Summer light
A large and delicate
Presence, groping along meadow and stones—
The young man leaned on a broken wall,
Tapping tapping his riding crop.

His name was William Adams *taptap,*
And I crushed green leaves,
A surge of sea in my ears.
My name *taptap,* what was my name...

My name is Ellen White, I said,
A sea singing at my back,
Combers tossing sirens, mermaids, whistling fish—
My name is Ellen Cameron White, I called
Over noise of surf, scent of green,
My name, my name is Ellen White.

3. Ellen Cameron: My Locket

Last night
The wake in Ash Grove,
Then home at daybreak.
Mother and Mrs. White
Scrubbed him on a dining table—
Our neighbors hid behind curtains—
No one came—
A white tin bowl, water rings, rag
Where captains peacocked over supper—

Others wept in an airless
Back bedroom. Not I—
I stood alone in the chamber—
There was a great press of air—
I drew back the sheet.

Mounted
To my throat, as if
To fly, escape, pursue,
And mate in air,
My soul had grown
Too large for flesh.

So this is a man,
—Sweetheart, husband-not-to-be—
This skin of silk and callus, dead
Throne of chest,
Marble of unmoving
Legs, unchilded sex.
So he is come
To this, all spirit flown, what's left
No better than a slab of meat
Wrapped against the bloody-minded flies.

Mother had torn his blouse, trimming
Stiffened cloth close to black gouts.
With a kitchen knife, I hacked
Curls from his nape,
Tying one
With a thread yanked from my skirt.

Faint fire of shots—
Dried blood and wellwater
Sloshing in a bowl—
Cries, mine, springing off like birds
Flushed from scrub—
Some sounds I shall never be rid of, not in a long
Calendar of years
As I gaze at wavering
Selves mirrored in the steel glass,
A girl, a woman, a crone-to-be.
She's wearing gifts
—Combs of silver, burnished locket—
And still retains the tinder of his love.
Ah! There! Wasn't that a smoldering
And tongue of flame against her fingertips?
No, no, the letters have gone cold,
Though passionate
And clasped in hands.
She's Ellen Cameron, not White.
That name will sleep with the unborn.
And Ellen Cameron is
Leaning, listening
To catch—there it is!—
The sound of a closing gold door.

LETTERS FROM ELSEWHERE

The final year they strayed to far
Edges, to where the continent
Decays and crumbles. Tidal surge
Ran wild in devil's kettlestones,
And kayak-shaped remains of seals
Struck thuddingly against the cliffs.
Feet stumbled on a rocky thrust
Potholed with pools of frayed rosettes,
Anemones that stirred in swirls
Or blinked and shrank abashed to buds.
And having then achieved the end
Of earth and found just echoings
To drawn-out plains within, he failed.
Or elsewhere, lapse more casual, drowned
By mist in salmonberry scrub.
That fall he sought a place alone,
And having claimed it, said that Claire
Was trenched more deeply in his dreams,
A picture locked inside a chest,
A wardrobe's snowy wraithlike dress.
His testaments were paper: crisp,
They cut. But Claire had gone a world
Beyond the South where they knew home,
The thicket, gale, and battling trees.
She wouldn't play a windswept girl
Who stared from dark, disordered lawns
While mansion lights made promises.
Though numb, she sought internal thaw.
She hunkered in the wilderness
And met a demon on the sands.
She climbed to flamey mountaintops
And trembled at the burning sun,
Enduring metamorphosis.

LIVING IN A DEAD FRIEND'S HOUSE

In memory of AJP

He's gone, and still this godly fingerwork
   of mount and grass and star is worth a psalm.

A great ox-bow of mountain crests the sky,
   the same as days when Claire was seventeen

And climbed a slope with other girls to hear
   her teacher's voice in vanished lilt and fall.

When Claire remembers the machinery
   of him, the smitten heart, violets not sent,

When she takes note of him, he's strangely young.
   Then she is older, after all. Alive.

What was he that she should be so mindful?
   Majestic child, alone, adorned with dream?

He mused—his youth heartstruck beside the founts
   Of jessamine—on Lawrence's women,

Gave heed to suppleness, the tender horns
   Of moonflowers, the languidness of girls.

How is it that, he asked, these blossoms yield
   Whiteness to moon when no one looks but me?

One night a blur against the glass scared Claire,
   And her scare scared the rest. The girl is flown—

At night now she's rereading his frail gods,
   And would be glad to see a face at panes.

And when the wind dies off in shuffles, she
   Looks up, recalls the sound of shallow steps,

And like those elder ones upon the brink
   Of disbelief, Claire stands, imagines much—

Can spirit haunt the strongholds that it knew?
   She checks the door, hoping it might be true.

Narrative of a Buried Life

Claire, her song, no. 5

At first she grieved, then cast him off,
And we saw them no more on our
River of floating images.
A lover's green canoe dwindled
To small, oh, smaller: all the chance
To call it back was gone. A raft
Of portraits was secured in drawers.
The serious child's eyes and mouth,
So womanly, drank in the dark.
One time she spoke: *We are alone,*
We die alone. Our gossips claimed
She sealed her panes against the tunes
Of birds, the shouts of children. She
Wished to prepare, we said, alone
To keep a silent watch, to wait
For her last hour. No flowery branch,
No gleaming story passed her door,
And only trembling light on sills
Recalled our flowing picture-stream.
Yet had she asked, we could have told
From our own stories' downward drift
Or from our children, over whom
A frail and somber moonlight broods,
That He would be awaiting her,
Always, as patient as a straight-
Back chair, the very straightest chair
In all the numberless

A RETREAT

It was a scape of giants, skirl and lash
Of centuries old creatures. Whirl and clash

Of soldiering plum trees, each tortured limb
Propped by a scabby crutch. A garden Grimm,

The vegetable head of boxwood flopped
Apart, its empty heart first bored, then stopped

By shadbush saplings. In the still green socket
Claire talked with her old love, and gathered pocket

Amulets—lucky buckeyes, buffed and brown
And big—the stones to deck a Green Man's crown.

And crossing crystal tails of snow, they looked
Until it seemed the goblin setting brooked

No further staring, no more saying save
Goodbye, and nothing doing but to wave,

To kiss and part, to have no more of *they*.
Claire watched the blue bug skittering away

Downhill, and waved until it was quite gone,
Then turned her face to greet the monstrous lawn,

A woman slim and small to meet such scale.
Determined just the same, she did not quail,

Her hand upon the lion-headed lock
But glanced about just once at cairns of rock

And wrecks of arbors, lifting up her gaze
To see a nest of rubbish ride the maze

Of breeze and bough, where rotten slats of wing
Battered the air and beat toward breathless spring.

CROFT WITH COWS

A former guest left tinder—fiery notes
That Claire pondered, and after saw all things
With warm romantic gaze. The tiny motes
Of flies, the cindered pith of fir that clings

To earth as landmark of decay, the slough
Of corrugated mud around a trough—
Though in the mucked-up scene was nothing new,
She liked the ricks and beasts, the homely croft.

The cows came billowing through cloud to loom
Or flop behind the fence. Their mouths a-steam,
They ground in rhythm, fed a bag of moon.
If milked in early spring they'd strain the gleam

Of buds and snow-drops, cowslips in a pail.
But hold on now, these weren't—Claire crowed out loud—
Moon goddesses, la-lyrical and pale
But clumps of sodden steers who never wowed

The girls—their corm of manhood cropped, bellows
Long past. "No mammoth snacks," Claire thought to warn,
But most kept chewing; some other fellows
Slipped one by one into the darkened barn.

Sea Change

Sidewinding crab and sleepy snail
Are moored on ribbon grass

As bending, swaying, Claire's first love
Scoops fossils out of marsh,

And strands of bubbles foam around
His feet. Her sneakers flow

With pearls, she bends to carve their names
On dimpled sand. Elsewhere,

On other shores fish roil in waves,
Razored by shell and glass,

And lovers' names silt up. He takes
A flute—once pelican—

And plays, while ibis fly above
In crooked, wishbone V.

A lover's heavy wrists belie
The fragile, bird-like song.

And Claire goes hollow, whistling—fresh
Islands aglint with stars

That taste like salt of youthful tears
Arise from ocean's bed.

WINDOWMAKER

Claire, her song, no. 6

Remember when
I pieced the glass
For Cuthbert's nave?
I storied round
Strawbed and throne,
Set blaze to wings,
Praised Him with star
And shark and stone.
The glass glistered
Like flaming twigs
Kindled in hands.
Where has the fire
Flickered and flown—
What pleases glass
In gilded arcs
When flesh once wick
Is chill as wax?

At night I dream
My own glass kings,
But lead can't hold—
The fragments spring
To starry space,
And leave a gap
On night and cold.
At dawn I wake
In my old place,
Nothing awry,
In glass my face,
At dusk and noon
The same. My feet
Pass by pale dead
And buried fame,
Go soft on stone
Cut with her name.

LETTER

Limbs on a grate broke asunder,
And for an instant Claire could hear
The talk of thunder—after-spill
Of glow and tumble made a song
Of silvery, wind-shaken chimes.
The days of pour had soaked her scene—
The little coves, the laurel balds,
The Tuckasegee gorged with silt,
Her mother's slope deluged with bloom.

At dusk Claire chewed her pen and dreamed
Of forty days of ark and flood,
Of smelling Noah's sharpened stink,
Bedraggled quills and splattered hides
Scorching her nose. A dove down-gyred
Through skeins of fairest, final drops.
But this had been a four days' storm,
And afterward, no rainbowed Word.

"My friend," she wrote, "last night the storm
Seemed cave, a mighty-arched retreat,
Though rumbles traveled from nearby
Where mudslides sealed our Balsam Gap
And flash floods bucked the local bridge."
She paused, then added, "Is it true
We dance on slickened trestle tracks
All careless of the coming freight
And downward sickle's streaming arc?
Last night I dreamed a drowning sleep
At river's very center, dreamed
That tear-streaked mountains ranged in rings
Around me, giant mourning girls.
But cloudbursts rose to lash their flanks,
And with the arms of swollen creeks
In torrents strove to bring them down."

In April

On school vacation, Claire flew home to small
Discovery—above the bed, Chagall,

A tacked print, *Le Poete Allonge.* Its song,
Its shades marred slumber. Nights, she scribbled long

Confessions: "Friend," she wrote, "this picture drifts
Through sleep, engenders ghosts that flow from rifts

In arctic plains—midnight, the poet poled
Into my sight. He steered an ice floe foaled

From bergs—another sleep, before the dawn,
He charted islands, and, half-sauced, a pawn

To drink, compared the death of cells that slip
From sodden brains to polar tears that drip

From massive glacial fields. He cast a spell
With boasts and tales about his camps, the fell

Crevasse of Fallen Men, Deceitful Land,
The North and South Furies, Defeated Strand.

He is my dream. And chambers me. His thought
Ripples, *aurora borealis* caught

Within a skull, and brightens, pole star sure.
Last night my dreaming sky—sleet-laden, pure—

Reminded him of *The Snow Queen,* how Kay's
Cold shards spelled out ETERNITY—the blaze

Of freedom charged the world with rosy spring—
And when he fell to rest within the ring

Of arms (my drowsing arms), I saw a realm
All rime-decked pinnacles, and how at helm

Of sled dog dreams he'd crossed vast latitudes
Of unknown lands to please the heart that broods."

Becoming Landscape

One summer Claire and her mother were trapped,
Inside a dusty home without a man
As slowly porches filled with ashen leaves
And twilight. They imagined bodies marred
By growth of children. And became two sweet
Old-fashioned sisters, keepsake roses pressed
In *Little Women*. Claire was Beth, that girl
Who looped her gentle arms around a neck,
Then kissed and kissed until the blood appeared.
In autumn she was smaller than before,
Still trying to believe a stranger's words,
The stories she re-read in his notebooks,
But sure they'd please another woman's eye.
Come winter, Claire reclaimed a single cell
Within a dream, her castle far away:
Three towers, one six-sided, bells, and glass—
A leaded Mary rising over stairs
And thorny roses in a Coat of Arms.
Alone with spring, she bent beneath a lamp,
A stream of cobalt bubbling from her pen.

Intent, she wrote, "So how much does it take
For you to be just part of landscape, Claire—
A mute, accepted doorway at the end
Of woods and the alerted animals?"

AFTER RAIN

Past a sourwood grove and cities of bees,
Claire wandered, asking, *Will I*
Always be this lonely,
A flowering tree the bees
Do not seek? Will I
Always be beginning, stalled
By surfaces of things?
Over ridges the sky divided mauve
And blue, while cloudlets softened backs
Of mountain ranges, showed the distances
Between. Fishing out her book, Claire penned:
It's a beginning,
And to whitewashed warehouses
Above the orchards
Is lent dignity of age
And prosperity.
At her back the scattered bee-boxes gleamed,
As shining as a hope of heaven, stored
With light. Damp flowers of sourwood lured the bees.
And Claire wrote. *It's white again with mist*
Where highways merge with earth—pale Cherokee
Beadwork, spirit of rain, feather of spume.

Claire: in the beginning.

A Winter's Tale

And Claire returned
To pace a room where sun
Threw glowing rings of light—resolved
To be a watcher of the leaves, no more
To spy on men.

She'd gone to look
At waves where in the spring
A skiff capsized—the boy was drowned,
While on near shores the watchers made immense
But silent signs.

The boy revolved,
The colored maple leaves
Struck water, sank past open hands.

Linnet and thrush
Bore Claire away on sweep
Of currents. Watchers wrote to her
Each night but didn't know the secret place
To leave their notes.

In dreams she spoke
To them: "I know your names.
In morning when the light would flare
On ice in Blackstone Park, you thought I walked
Among the trees,

Afar, my hair—
Well, you were wrong. It must
Have been the rosy dawn you dreamed,

Who walked among
Auroral trees the way
She walked three thousand years ago.
Claire said: I'll tell you how my image has
Receded, lost

Herself in firs,
And journeyed steadily

With thrush and singing linnet—changed
So she no longer knows your names. You'll glimpse
A girl and boy

On colder days.
They run through woods, embrace
To warm each other—but cannot

     Because
     Their hearts are
     Snow: mine is snow."

ENCHANTED STORY

"What's the point in just describing?" Claire asks
Her book. "That's work a sharp apprentice does.
And what about a voice, its singing tasks,
Its natural lilt and sway—what of the buzz

Of story? Let her yack about the cloister
Of childhood, how the girl unwarped the all
Her holy mother taught—began to hoist her
Unruly self on hands and knees, to crawl

Or pray—and how she dragged her dreadlocked hair
Upsidedown on a prong of mop if she's
Come to that pass. And let her learn an air
Of ease in making—makers must to please

A watching eye, and have her deal with seeds
And atoms, planets, oceans, stars and bread,
Old ballads, nursery songs, and fairy deeds,
The bridal tales where world begins with red

In stains of blood on snow. And she should make
A fable from that fall, a myth from milk
That fetters babes, a tale from wars that break
Her women, children, men, the common ilk,

A poem from the flush of middle age
Before age, when she prunes her spirit back
Into a crone more clearly she: a sage,
A witch as squat and piping as a black-

Hearted stove, a godmum of gifts and cast
Godspells. She'll charm a legend from the round
Of days and swansongs from the flying last,
Then draw a life within, without a sound."

Barbarians Among Us

Claire, her song, no. 7

In languid gardens, images
Made sparse and whitened—more asleep
Than teacups stacked, the bowls face down—
Barbarians were slow as stone
And more at rest than close-furled fans.
Their soft, incessant poets saw
Our home motifs—the laureled hair-
Of-Daphne, bear, and iron wolf—
As florid, sundering air with shock.
Our bold and lovely bronze was stored
In armories, our bellied jars
Were glutted, packed with silt the wind
Had tossed from tireless east to west.
They wished to sift our bones with sleep.
Yet we—unruly natives—stabbed
Rebellious flags in flanks of sand
And jumbled air with many prayers.
And often we detected signs,
Forbidden flourish of pan pipes
Or hair-of-Daphne chalked on doors,
And laughed or cried, as was outlawed.

ASKED OF A SIBYL

Claire, her song, no. 8

Birthed with the mask of wisdom on her face,
And cauled by light, she sprang with goat-legged grace

Across her native pastures, known to cairns
Where buried rulers waned, the Stone Age barns

Of boulders, giant-built, the careless cache
Where snub, forgotten gods were strewn like trash.

She drove the swine and sang of passing days
And times to come. A poet chanted lays

Of wine and rose, but after many stairs
And beds and well-kissed hems—too many airs

Of love on lyres—and after laurel wreaths
Aplenty, withering—he was with leaves

Well pleased. The pigherd child, the place seemed simple,
Uplifted boughs of green the only temple,

And switch in hand she cried her dream of truth.
Oracular, and yet, no grief, no ruth

Had touched the heart so wholly bound to fount
And quarry, rock and cavern, vale and mount.

On fire with mortal flames, the poet sang
And singing asked—could she resist the clang

Of call, the knowing, when on hills and moors
The sibyl trod so near its radiant doors?

CLAIRE THINKS OF EDVARD'S DREAMS

1. The Lonely Ones

A face like a dried leaf
Warned Claire: remember how
A man's a door that shuts
Against a meadow's spring
Of loosening gold, and how
Mirages glint with salt
And cannot hold, how you
Shrink and fade with distance.

All heedless, Claire went in.
The edges lifted. Reeds
Defined the water. Clean
Paths led into whiteness.

Mirages warmed her face.
Light filled the downy trees.

2. Self-portrait at 2:00 A.M.

A staircase that climbs
For seven years, a black door,
Red door, the empty room.

Mirrors,
Limpid squares which box
Ovals of his face.

In well water
A white O
Stricken by eyes, nose, mouth.

Small signs of love carved
On hands talk
Fast, falling like peels
From fruit.

At night he seeks the places
Which move like sores
Within, wrapping
Wounds with scenes of desire.
A road separates two
Figures like a flat
Answer, his friends
Exit in a yellow boat.

He presses his face
Open against the dark,
His consuming bed,
The window's last
Lucent
Eye.

About the Turn of the Leaf

Yellow women with mauve shawls
Shaken over shoulders,
The clicking steps of pencilled women—
Flakes of gold leaf
Surround them when they turn.
Claire follows, gazes in a door
(Leaves, edges
Sharp behind muslin curtains,
A small-calved dancer
Preening at glass).
A red dress shines,
And Claire looks in passing
At twined and twinned sisters, at painted
And slick-skinned fruit.
By the path are posers,
Sweet like a crowd of maples
(Rooted, flecked with red,
The balanced sap
Tilted and changed).
Women yield,
Dropping gingko-leaf fans.
Abstracted they droop over a river, reflective,
Romantic and soft where a current sways
And, where still, precise.
Gleaned stems of light hold back autumn rains—
And Claire, that sprig and leafy spray of youth?
For today she expands, putting forth
A few leaves, each green as springtime,
Each touched with bloodspot.

Childbed

Claire bent to look and whispered, "That is all,
It's nothing but a grainy photograph.
It's not our place, nor anywhere I know."
A larch was flowing from the earth to cloud;
The pictured cows were bowed to slanted sleet.
They were a piece of winter's puzzle, drab
And difficult, with sheds and tools and shack
Repeating seasonal monotony.
Claire told a tale about it—chinks of light
Were twinkling, calling, even knew her name.
The girl who slipped the curtain back to peep
Was watching for the man who hauled a babe
Gone blue with cold inside his doctor's bag.
"And she is me," Claire mused. "I was the one
By windows, always longing for the new
And magical to be released by birth."
But in a rear bedroom, the mother moaned,
Forgot the whoop and thrust of life, the babe
Who lay spring-coiled and struggling to be born.
The woman's mind was set adrift to freeze
On arctic floes of stark and piled-up sheets.
All through the cave of house, stalactites wept
The tears of ice that carpeted the boards
With pearl—behind the child, stalagmite trees
And ice-plants swelled to thicket, forest, bars
Uncrossable. "Don't turn your head," Claire willed,
"Just stay like this forever, eyes on lights
Like stars approaching. Fix them on the man
And on a bag in which the living boy
Is pressing headfirst toward the cloudy day,
His every breathless pulse a miracle."

PRESAGE

Claire, her song, no. 9

A woman shelters in her parents' house
But hears demands from miles away where love
Guns down highways, pausing indecisive
At crossroads markers reading Cherokee
Atlanta, Bryson City, Franklin, Clyde.
Each year's like this: a car's released from earth
To ricochet off Jarrett's cobblestones
As boys awaken to a dream of death
And one, kindled and curled in wreckage, burns.
The railroad gleams and whips its trestled light
Around the hills in speed past bounds he knew.
On Main a girl is watching. Boys and pups
Shift feet and lean into a farm truck's sway—
They seem as brothers, kinned, the hair and manes
Alive, their growth almost detectable.
Each spring it happens so: some older boy
Goes wild in balsam groves or graveyard shade
Behind a Baptist church, in seats of cars.
The boy drives fast and thrusts abortions off
To Atlanta. By noon she cries, released.
A rocky wall preserves its honored dent,
The boys and hounds run free on pasture slopes,
New green retakes the mountainsides, and buds
Appear like gnats above the icy streams.
Each time the same. It's spring, and someone has
Grown careless of our ancient auguries
That read in stones the coldness of the grave,
That see in shade of trees a deeper shade,
And prophecy the reaper's crooked blade.

ABANDON

Substance of evening comes, remorseless blue
And far more dense than it had seemed before.
Able to bear the moon? One might well sue

The sky for answers, for the moon, once just
A marble—aggie, milky end-of-day
Glass—nothing! taw forgotten in the dust—

Is truly marble and is liable,
So looming-great and ponderous it seems,
To fall. The experts aren't reliable

And cannot vouch. But each in her own room,
Forgotten dolls tremble as Claire's toy house,
Half tilted to one side and deep in gloom

Of grass, now raises its unguarded face,
Desirous, faint beneath the wind's fine strokes.
The breezes swell, and violet airs now race

To pelt the tiny house with darts of brush.
Antic, electrical beasts brisk and yowl.
The baby gasps and drowns in shadows. *Hush*.

PIANO RAG

Claire, her song, no. 10

A mangled key
Inside a lock,
The deadbolt thrown.
In curls of leaf
And dusty light
Tinkles music,
Calliope
Ragtime—a child
Leaps up to dance.

A setting sun
Is glittering,
Strikes the record
And scatters lights
That wheel in wings
Above her head—
The turning child
Looks up and stares
And laughs in glee.

A childish head
Bobs in shadows
But sees the shine,
Sees feathers float
As broken rain-
Bows arc in rings.
A needle lifts
And drops, begins.
A child begins.

We beat on glass,
Watch orbitals
Of rainbow, beat
Against the time
When on ceilings
Resembling bright
Angelic skies,
Figures decline
And the lights fail.

Upon the First Bathtub in Collins, Georgia

Despite his fears of sisters' nymph-like wiles,
Girls needle naked on the ornate tiles,

Claire's carpenter grandfather rolled his ark
Of porcelain inside. Below, in dark

And cool were claws immarbled with the prize,
Tight-seized, of four white aggies, giant size.

The spilled gardenia powder scented air
And dusted fronds of black-stemmed maidenhair;

A woman clutched by heels her last mistake.
The baby chortled at the tub-bound lake,

And grabbed maternal arms once thought beyond
All birth. But Lila late was granted bond

Of motherhood—with figs and grapes the land
Rejoiced, with tub and well fresh-dug in sand.

Her children shadowed past the open door,
Arms dipping cloths and splattering the floor

With purple slops. The rags of world new cleansed,
They put off gowns and—frugal sisters—rinsed

In baby's cloudy bath, waving their arms
And lifting necks of swans, displaying charms

Of flight or the savanna poise of wings
At rest—the lure of wild and childish things,

Heartbeating loveliness of dead and dear
Who glide with upheld heads across the mirror.

THE LOCOMOTIVE SONG

At Collins, in the sultry afternoon
The clan stood round the pump to eat fresh figs,
A whistle coming low from far away.
The uncles laughed and told the kids: *there's Jo!*
And eyed Aunt Jo with sweet fig in her mouth—

Hibiscus-shaded nights in Gramercy,
Claire Ann lay sprawled in bed, the sheets thrown off,
Awake to hear the tremulous sound flower
And widen in moonshine, as glory neared—
Its brute earthquake uprooting room and world.
She leaped up to the shaking windowsill
And watched the midnight's cone of light sweep by—

Savannah noons, the freights clicked past, with chants
Of *Southern Serves the South* and *Southern Serves
The South,* with cool jazz notes set in between.
And Claire Ann was the child with long fair braids—
Waving and waving to the engineers
Who hit the whistle high and bittersweet,
And afterward to the caboose's boy,
Bandanna waving like a loco flag—

In Georgia nights she heard a song in bass
From railyards, laughs and shouts of railroad men
Hooking and unhooking heavy boxcars,
And then a rumble back to rhythm—beat
Beginning slowly, *Southern Serves the South,*
Then quickly song wailed out—cars flew the rails,
At Claxton stopped to load Christmas fruitcake
Or sweet Vidalia onions, cotton, coal—

She'd scramble down the snaky banks of home
As early as they'd set her free, yet not
So very soon—a whitehot disk of sun
Already burning dew from morning rails—
And Claire Ann teetered, balancing, arms out,
Choo-chooing like a Chattanooga train,
Rejoicing in the day, in iron that gleamed

And pointed like an arrow, gold and bronze,
And where the locomotive's wheels had rolled,
She still could feel a ringing on the rails—

History Report

In Delaware, attired in homemade pink,
The homesick Claire Ann read her cards aloud—
How combine teeth, with one smooth motion pulled
A migrant's ponytail out by its crowd

Of roots. (Her father shoved off from the South,
And in a Kansas yard her hair was shorn.
Remains of ten years' braided hair still shine
Preserved in cellophane.) The time was morn,

Class met outside. Before a clipped backdrop
Of topiary shrubs the shade was cold.
And after school, when walking slowly up
The highway to the rented house, she told

The air in whispers: *Migrant girl,*
The yellowed grass on barren breadth
Of empty city lots is gleaned
From your anonymous small death.

Testament of the Paisley Loom-Workers

> ... who starved to death in the famine of 1877 to
> 1879. Their sensitive hands, attuned to the loom,
> were too fine for any other form of work.
>> —R. & T. Kovel

Claire, her song, no. 11

Their only solace, letting fingers stray
In rain. Was there no job for idle hands
But prayer? No harp, asleep inside a silk
Mitten? No sweet cascade of strings? As child,
Our Mr. Edwards, famous priest, conceived
The purest soul as skeins of countless threads,
A Loom of Being. Paisley weavers wrought
Kashmiri birds and foreign flowers, dreamed
An earthly heat of generation, died,
The mother, father, baby gripping toy
With agile hands. If there had been a space
In Old or New-found Worlds, between the tides
Of carpet-bagging, Franco-Prussian wars,
And rise of factories, to pause and mourn,
To cry, *dear Christ, now halt the loss of all
That's feckless-fine!* we might have been redeemed.

FORT HAYS, KANSAS

They lived in a pink house.
The father went to work
While the mother tied a scarf over her hair.
Dirt sifted under doors and windows.
She swept the floors
And sewed. Late at night from a room
Papered with pine needles
And juniper berries,
Claire Ann could hear her depress
The foot pedal. A motor raced,
A tiny light shone.

Weekends they always
Traveled on a straight road out of town,
First stopping at barbed wire
Where they saw buffalo
Gather in bunches by a lean-to,
One old bull rubbing up against planks.
The wind pushed tufts of fur
Across a wallow and dying grass.

Sixty miles or more farther west
And the landscape beginning to change,
The father's eye
Fastened to a moving
Point on a road's horizon.
The day was, as always, half
Ruined—this time by the mother, who tried
To pick a cactus blossom near the road,
Then hid her swollen hand.
A hundred miles farther on,
The land had grown up around them,
And the father sang his three songs,
Beginning with "Lonesome Pine."

THE CHERRY TREES

But no salt glaze
Could be so delicately cracked
As were that morning's holly leaves,
Each shelled in ice. The cherry stones
Still linked to trees, the hips and barbs
Of rose arbors, the spiral threads
On Adam's Needle clung to clear
Remarks of ice.

The scatterings
Made glints on garden paths—and there
A daughter paced the night to dawn,
Her fingers curled around the word
That came toward her, that made of her
Morning's mourner.

By ice, by air
A cherry tree's meshwork of boughs
Is doubled, lined beyond the bark
As though a painter's ruthless brush,
Had passed along each crook and curve,
Each curve of air beside a curve.
Meanwhile a body yielded ghost,
The timelines on a face grew stiff,
And eyes stared up as final puffs
Of breath were pilfered.

It was a day
Of sober cloud. The girl Claire Ann
Who played in knotted garden beds
Came to the mourner, as if she
Could feel a stranger's grief and gave
—What did the child intend to give?—
A winter cherry, ancient flesh
Enfolded, sucked around the pit.
Her hand was open, small. Her hand
Was wet with ice. As if she said,
Grave-eyed, *This very fruit I plucked*
And saved to mark your father's death.
The eldest trees must yield to seed
And bear the stone.